YOUR KNOWLEDGE HAS VALUE

- We will publish your bachelor's and master's thesis, essays and papers

- Your own eBook and book - sold worldwide in all relevant shops

- Earn money with each sale

Upload your text at www.GRIN.com and publish for free

Bibliographic information published by the German National Library:

The German National Library lists this publication in the National Bibliography; detailed bibliographic data are available on the Internet at http://dnb.dnb.de .

This book is copyright material and must not be copied, reproduced, transferred, distributed, leased, licensed or publicly performed or used in any way except as specifically permitted in writing by the publishers, as allowed under the terms and conditions under which it was purchased or as strictly permitted by applicable copyright law. Any unauthorized distribution or use of this text may be a direct infringement of the author s and publisher s rights and those responsible may be liable in law accordingly.

Imprint:

Copyright © 2017 GRIN Verlag
Print and binding: Books on Demand GmbH, Norderstedt Germany
ISBN: 9783668678460

This book at GRIN:

https://www.grin.com/document/417202

Marcel Strangmueller

"Why they are wrong". Analyzing globalization and its impact on the rich and poor

GRIN Verlag

GRIN - Your knowledge has value

Since its foundation in 1998, GRIN has specialized in publishing academic texts by students, college teachers and other academics as e-book and printed book. The website www.grin.com is an ideal platform for presenting term papers, final papers, scientific essays, dissertations and specialist books.

Visit us on the internet:

http://www.grin.com/

http://www.facebook.com/grincom

http://www.twitter.com/grin_com

Why they are wrong – Anti-globalists

Globalisation is a highly opinionated topic, which is discussed throughout the years (Boddy 2014), especially since Donald Trump won the election in 2016 who is now promoting a way of business which is considered to be more in the direction of protectionism rather than globalisation (Berenson 2016). Protectionism is supposed to protect producers, workers and businesses of the import-competing sector from other countries. Political tools to achieve such a protection of national business are tariffs, regulations on imported goods and other government regulations (Milner 1989). This is against what the world has been moving towards in the past decades since WWII. Western society since then has promoted a more global approach of living, including migration, trade and problem solving (Bardham 2017).

Globalisation is described as the process of increasing the integration of internationally dispersed goods (Boddy 2014, Banerjee et al. 2009). These integrations include factors such as culture, society and economical, political and informational co-operation (Linsted 2009). All those factors contribute to the fact that the world is moving closer together rather than further away, how Donald Trump is suggesting. The world is becoming a "global village" (Linsted 2009, p.341) with products available in countries that do normally not have access to them, such as bananas in the UK or a Mercedes in the United States.

Critics of globalisation suggest that globalisation as it is today only benefits the rich and leaves out the poor and defenceless (BBC 2017). To assess the extent to which this argument is true this essay will discuss the topic of globalisation with a view on the article published by The Economist in October 2016 "Why they´re wrong" (The Economist 2016, p.13). It will start with definitions of rich and poor and when someone is considered rich or poor and when a country is considered rich or poor. This is because everyone has an opinion about what is means to be rich, but these vary a great deal throughout society. Further it will assess negative impacts on the poor and how they are hurt by the process of globalisation and positive impacts on the richest countries and people and the ways they benefit from a more globalised world. To finish the essay off, it will consider how being part of the "global village" positively impacts the poor and why globalisation is a good process for all.

Over the years there is a vast variety of definitions and descriptions about at what point a person is rich or poor. To be able to argue precisely this essay will go with Kaplinski´s (2005) definition in which he takes the World banks PPP $ in consideration. He describes someone poor with the inability to sustain appropriate shelter and the ability to access food over a long period of time. The UN (2017) and Kaplinski (2017) stipulate on the fact that a person living under 2 PPP$ per day is considered poor. The PPP stands for Purchasing Power Parity and is translates the currency in to US$ to be able to compare countries´ inhabitants purchasing power. Other comparisons were the Mars-Index or the McDonalds Index where items on were compared and it was looked at how much could be purchased with the same amount of money. If the essay refers to poor people in the following it will refer back to the 2 PPP$ line, under which they live.

While the UN and the World Bank agree on a clear line of people being poor there is no internationally valid level of when someone is rich. Therefore if the essay mentions rich people it will refer to people on the highest level of taxation in the United States, which kicks in at a yearly income of 415,051 US$ (bankrate 2017). The reason the United States are chosen as a comparison in this segment, is due to the fact that the article in the centre of this discussion uses the US frequently as an example and it is considered the leader of the Western world (The Economist 2016).

Following the definitions of people is the definition on when a country is considered poor or developing. Therefore a combination of the World Bank´s (2017) and the UN´s (2017) definitions will be used to be able to describe the differences between rich and poor countries. The World Bank has converted the local currency for each country and put them into a list that splits developed (rich), transition (medium) and developing (poor) countries in a way that can be applied globally. Following the World Bank´s and UN´s listings countries that are developed at the current moment qualify when they have a GNI (Gross National Income) of 12,615$ per capita or above, which means that every national´s income is bringing money in to the country is considered no matter where the income is generated. Poor (developing) countries on the other hand are considered to be that, when their GNI is below 1,035$ GNI per capita (World Bank 2017, UN 2017). The poorest countries in the world are clustered in Africa, Asia and Africa and are the ones that are considered developing or just reached the bottom end of the transition phase and this is what the essay will refer to as poor countries (Bardham 2017, Hill and Hernandez-Requejo 2011).

In the following the essay will discuss negative impacts globalization has on the poor people of the poor countries and on the poor or unskilled workers in the developed countries. Donald Trump argues that due to globalisation American workers are losing their jobs and unemployment rates are rising (Wilts 2017). He is blaming most of that on the Chinese and other Asian countries with low labour costs. While most of his accusations are wrong, he is right with the fact that low skilled work is often outsourced into countries where labour cost and employment law are not as developed as they are in the US or other Western countries (Kang´ethe 2014). This is due to the massive difference in cost for corporations in manufacturing and other companies focusing on producing goods with a large low skilled workforce. This is in fact hurting the poor and helping the rich, as suggested by critics, in a way that it takes away income in America, raises unemployment levels and generates more profit for already massive corporations, such as NIKE or Apple who outsource most of their production to Asia (Apple 2017, Nike 2017).

However, while those outsourcing operations come in cost of jobs in the domestic market, they generate a large amount of labour for host countries, making it possible to decrease their unemployment rate and raise the standard of living there (Boddy 2014, Banerjee et al. 2009, Hill and Hernandez-Requejo 2011). Bardham (2017) further adds that globalisation was the key driver of decreasing mass poverty in the Asian market, as even though so called "Sweat Shops" (Bardham 2017) have a low standard of health and safety as well as low wages (compared to Western countries), they pay their workers more for their work, than they would earn in other comparable and local businesses.

Nevisky (2017) found out that foreign investment could lead to a boost of the local economy, because of the generation of jobs related to globalisation (Oldford and Olchere 2016). Baylee (2016) argues that multi-national corporations, expanding into new markets, pay their workers up to 40% more than they would earn in comparable businesses in the local market. The arguments presented by Nevisky (2017) and Baylee (2016) show a strong argument for globalisation opposing the views of protectionists such as Trump or other closed nations of the world. While in the short-term labour is lost in countries whose corporations chose to outsource operations, in the long-term jobs are generated and the workforce is able to specialise in sectors that are supported by the country´s infrastructure and politics (Hill and Hernandez-Requejo 2011). So while there is an apparent short-term loss for poor people in industrialised countries, in the long-term jobs are created throughout the world including the domestic and international market.

Critics of globalisation use other arguments frequently, which include economical dangers within and between countries and how those economical factors impact politics and society (Linsted 2009, Bardham 2017). Due to globalisation markets are more connected than ever (Boddy 2014) and therefore their economies are as well. Because of that there is a danger coming from the risk of international economical recession (Hill and Hernandez-Requejo 2011). This was to be observed when in 1997 the baht in Thailand dropped and unemployment rose by 50% within that decade (Bardham 2017). The recession mainly happened due to speculative investments from Western countries into the baht, which was not able to react properly to those and resulted in a massive decline.

However, investment into and acquisitions of Asian companies can bring an economical upswing to the market (Oldford and Olchere 2016, Asongu 2014). With their study Oldford and Olchere (2016) discovered that cross-country acquisitions can have very positive effects on the economy and because of the connectedness of markets, this upswing can spread just as a recession can spread (Linsted 2009, Bardham 2017). Acquisitions of companies often result in higher wages for employees in the host country and the positive development of their working environment. Due to the internationality of the business after the acquisition, the workforce often feels more motivated and is then able to improve its efficiency, creating a positive impact on performance and ultimately on the GDP/GNI of the country (Oldford and Olchere 2016).

On the other side of the positive effects international investment, stands the fact that investments into new areas and exploration of new markets can cause host employees to lose their jobs and raise unemployment numbers in the area (Boddy 2014, Bardham 2017). This can be observed when corporations such as Starbucks or McDonalds expand their business into new areas of the world. For example Starbucks often pushes small local coffee shops out of business, which cannot compete with the large corporation and its brand recognition (Boddy 2014). This can possibly increase poverty in those regions. In addition to pushing locals out of their jobs, corporations such as Wal-Mart or Nestlé often influence the market for food in countries with a focus on agriculture, such as Latin America for example (Nevisky 2017, Bardham 2017, Berkeley 2003). One occasion a negative impact on the local workforce by those giant corporations was when they pushed down prices for bananas and made local small and medium farmers uncompetitive (Nevisky 2017). This caused a rise in poverty levels and was considered and shows that globalisation can hurt the poor drastically and making the rich profit from that loss.

Another influence the globalisation of markets has, is on the society of developing countries. As the other points there are good and bad factors that can be argued for in this debate. Here the negative influence will first show how the poor in developing and transition countries suffer from globalisation, to make the rich richer and then how societies all around the globe benefit from the advances due to globalisation.

In societies around Eastern Asia and in Africa trafficking and corruption is a strong negative influence on the countries (Linsted 2009, Bardham 2017). With the demand for labour by large and rich multi-national corporations that is rising consistently, the problem of trafficking is increasing. This is due to hopes people have in bad situations and areas, in which school attendance is low and healthcare is bad or even non-existent (Banerjee 2009, Linsted 2009). These hopes are exploited by traffickers who use those poor people to make them work in factories around the countries for low wages in unbearable conditions. Because traffickers make them dependent on the work and support, it is almost impossible for them to break free and make the most out of the positives of the globalised world (Linsted 2009).

On the other side of the argument is that internationalisation of countries and companies, societies improve and grow closer together (Hill and Hernandez-Requejo 2011). This is in terms of culture, where prejudices and stereotypes are questioned and erased, with women in high executive positions and friend- and partnerships between races removing racism step by step (Hill and Hernandez-Requejo 2011). Another way, that globalisation is improving societies in developing countries, is the healthcare that has been shared between countries with knowledge and technology, to which those developing countries would not have access to (Walby 2009, UN 2017). With this sharing of competencies and the globalisation of knowledge, there are significant improvements made, which cannot be argued with. Overall life expectancy has risen by 17 years since the 1980s (UN 2017) and diseases, which were killing hundreds of thousands each year, are under control now. Some examples for those diseases are tuberculosis, malaria, mumps and HIV, which has been shrinking over the years (Walby 2009). For children the infant mortality under 5 year olds has been cut drastically around the globe with international movements to improve access to hospitals and local healthcare. Kang´ethe (2014) argues as well that school attendance in developing countries has rising by 50% over the last two decades, giving more and more young people access to the global market and supporting globalisation and internationalisation. So even though there is still a long way to go to eradicate differences in the societies, improvements are made on a daily basis that make the life of the poor easier and show the positive impacts of globalisation (UN 2017).

To summarise the outcome of this discussion and to express an opinion on whether they are wrong as mentioned in the Economist article mentioned earlier (The Economist 2016). There are always two sides to an argument and the anti-globalisation movement is making valid points when they say that globalisation is hurting the poor of the world. This is true in generally poor and developing countries when is comes to working conditions and wages, the lack of healthcare in rural areas and the lack of access to schools for kids. But not only the poor countries of the world suffer. Even developed countries´ unskilled labour force is suffering because of the globalisation of the markets. Because labour costs are a lot cheaper in Asia and Africa many see their jobs being outsourced into those areas leaving many without occupation and no regular income.

However, globalisation is an irreversible process that started years back after WWII and is getting more and more important. While negative impacts often make the headlines, there are many positives that come from globalisation. One of them is the reduction of prejudices and racism between and within countries, when ethnic and religious groups mix and harmonise. Another important point is that healthcare is improving throughout the world lifting the average life expectancy by 17 years and cut a large chunk out of infant mortality, by sharing knowledge and technology. Besides those, a major economic advantage of globalisation is the ability to produce and offer cheap products and services which improve life in developed and developing countries, by giving everybody access to affordable clothing and groceries.

So while globalisation can have negative effects, the "global village" (Linsted 2009) is happening and everyone will have a part to play in it. So rather than working against it and denying the positives of globalisation, we should all focus on improving the negative aspects and create a better world. They are wrong if they say that globalisation only benefits the rich.

References

BANERJEE, S. B., CARTER, C. and CLEGG, S., 2009. Managing Globalisation. In: GALLIERS R. D. and CURRIE, W. *Oxford Handbook for Management*. Oxford: Oxford press, pp. 301-342.

BANKRATE., 2017. "2016-2017 Tax Brackets | Bankrate.com". 2017. [viewed 8 December 2017]. Available from: http://www.bankrate.com/finance/taxes/tax-brackets.aspx

ASONGU, S., 2014. "Globalization, (Fighting) Corruption and Development: How are These Phenomena Linearly and Nonlinearly Related in Wealth Effects?". *SSRN Electronic Journal*[online]. vol. , 41, no. , 3, pp. 346-369 [viewed 8 December 2017]. Available from: https://search.proquest.com/docview/1523660453?accountid=12269

BARDHAN, P., 2017. "Does Globalization Help or Hurt the World's Poor?" [online]. [viewed 8 December 2017]. Available from: https://eml.berkeley.edu/~webfac/bardhan/papers/BardhanDoesGlobalizationHelp.pdf

BBC., 2017. "Negative impacts of globalisation" [online]. [viewed 8 December 2017]. Available from: http://www.bbc.co.uk/schools/gcsebitesize/geography/globalisation/globalisation_rev5.shtml

BERENSON, T., 2016. "Donald Trump Wins the 2016 Election". *The Times* [online]. [viewed 8 December 2017]. Available from: http://time.com/4563685/donald-trump-wins/

BODDY, D., 2014. *Management*. 5th ed. Harlow [etc.]: Pearson.

"Difference between GNP, GDP and GNI". 2017. [viewed 8 December 2017]. Available from: https://www.economicshelp.org/blog/3491/economics/difference-between-gnp-gdp-and-gni/

HILL, C. and HERNÁNDEZ-REQUEJO, W., 2011. *Global business today*. 3rd ed. Boston [u.a.]: McGraw-Hill Irwin.

JANDT, F., 2015. *Introduction to Intercultural Communication*. 7th ed. Thousand Oaks: SAGE Publications.

KANG'ETHE, S., 2014. "Panacea and Perfidy of Globalisation as an Engine of Social Development in Developing Countries". *Journal of Human Ecology* [online]. vol. , 47, no. , 2, pp. 193-200 [viewed 8 December 2017]. Available from: http://www.krepublishers.com/02-Journals/JHE/JHE-47-0-000-14-Web/JHE-47-2-000-14-Abst-PDF/JHE-47-2-193-14-2493-Kangethe-S-M/JHE-47-2-193-14-2493-Kangethe-S-M-Tx[11].pdf

KAPLINSKY, R., 2005. *Globalization, poverty and inequality*. 1st ed. Cambridge [u.a.]: Polity.

LINSTEAD, S., FULOP, L. and LILLEY, S., 2009. *Management and organization*. 2nd ed. Basingstoke: Palgrave Macmillan.

MILNER, H., 1989. *Resisting protectionism*. 1st ed. Ann Arbor, Mich.: Umi Books on Demand.

MOLLOY, B., 2016. "Does Globalization Harm the Poor?" [online]. [viewed 8 December 2017]. Available from: https://tifwe.org/does-globalization-harm-the-poor/

NESVISKY, M., 2017. "Globalization and Poverty" [online]. [viewed 8 December 2017]. Available from: http://www.nber.org/digest/mar07/w12347.html

THE ECONOMIST., 2016. "Anti-globalists Why they're wrong" [online]. [viewed 8 December 2017]. Available from: https://www.economist.com/news/leaders/21707926-globalisations-critics-say-it-benefits-only-elite-fact-less-open-world-would-hurt

UNITED NATIONS., 2016. *Country classification*. Belgium: United Nations.

UNITED NATIONS., 2017. "Global Issues Overview" [online]. [viewed 8 December 2017]. Available from: http://www.un.org/en/sections/issues-depth/global-issues-overview/

WALBY, S., 2009. *Globalization and Inequalities: Complexity and Contested Modernities*. 1st ed. Sage Publications.

WITS, A., 2017. "Donald Trump seems to turn on China after day of praising country". *The Independent* [online]. [viewed 8 December 2017]. Available from: http://www.independent.co.uk/news/world/americas/us-politics/trump-china-america-first-speech-day-after-praise-trip-latest-a8048781.html

WORLD BANK., 2017. "Why use GNI per capita to classify economies into income groupings? – World Bank Data Help Desk" [online]. [viewed 8 December 2017]. Available from: https://datahelpdesk.worldbank.org/knowledgebase/articles/378831-why-use-gni-per-capita-to-classify-economies-into

YOUR KNOWLEDGE HAS VALUE

- We will publish your bachelor's and master's thesis, essays and papers

- Your own eBook and book - sold worldwide in all relevant shops

- Earn money with each sale

Upload your text at www.GRIN.com
and publish for free